DOGS SET IX

CATAHOULA LEOPARD DOGS

Joanne Mattern
ABDO Publishing Company

visit us at
www.abdopublishing.com

Published by ABDO Publishing Company, 8000 West 78th Street, Edina, Minnesota 55439. Copyright © 2012 by Abdo Consulting Group, Inc. International copyrights reserved in all countries. No part of this book may be reproduced in any form without written permission from the publisher. The Checkerboard Library™ is a trademark and logo of ABDO Publishing Company.

Printed in the United States of America, North Mankato, Minnesota.
062011
092011

 PRINTED ON RECYCLED PAPER

Cover Photo: Alamy
Interior Photos: Alamy pp. 9, 13, 19; AP Images p. 15; Glow Images pp. 17, 21;
    iStockphoto pp. 5, 7, 11

Editors: Megan M. Gunderson, BreAnn Rumsch
Art Direction: Neil Klinepier

Library of Congress Cataloging-in-Publication Data

Mattern, Joanne, 1963-
  Catahoula leopard dogs / Joanne Mattern.
      p. cm. -- (Dogs)
  Includes index.
  ISBN 978-1-61714-990-0
  1. Catahoula leopard dog--Juvenile literature. I. Title.
  SF429.C35M38 2012
  636.73--dc22
                        2011009105

CONTENTS

THE DOG FAMILY

Dogs are beloved in countries around the world. Scientists have shown these popular pets descended from wolves. Dogs and wolves both belong to the family **Canidae**. This name comes from the Latin word *canis*, which means "dog."

Some dogs still look like wolves. Yet others look very different from their ancestors. Dogs display a wide range of shapes, sizes, and colors. They are organized into more than 400 different **breeds**.

Thousands of years ago, people began to **domesticate** dogs. Today, dogs help people in many ways. They hunt and herd. They protect people and property from danger. Dogs are also great companions and loving family pets.

One special **breed** is the Catahoula leopard dog. These dogs are great at hunting and herding animals. They are also loyal family members.

The Catahoula leopard dog is also called the Louisiana Catahoula leopard dog, the Catahoula cur, the Catahoula hog dog, and the Catahoula hound.

Catahoula Leopard Dogs

There are several legends about the Catahoula leopard dog's history. Some believe this **breed** descended from large mastiffs, bloodhounds, and greyhounds brought to North America by the Spanish explorer Hernando de Soto.

After the Spanish left, Native American tribes took in the dogs that were left behind. These large dogs bred with Native American dogs and possibly red wolves. Later, they may have bred with Beaucerons brought to Louisiana by French settlers.

Originally, Native Americans used these dogs to hunt large game such as deer and bobcats. Settlers used them to manage herds of wild cattle and wild hogs.

Today, the **American Kennel Club (AKC)** has assigned the Catahoula leopard dog to its herding group. However, it is not yet a fully recognized **breed** in the AKC.

This breed gets its name from the Catahoula Lake in Louisiana.

What They're Like

Catahoula leopard dogs are very smart. They like to investigate new situations. And, they are good at search and rescue jobs. So, Catahoulas are often used in law enforcement.

This **breed** has a lot of energy! Catahoulas need plenty of exercise and space to run. So, they should not be kept in apartments or homes with small yards.

Catahoula leopard dogs get along well with their families. They are very protective. So, it might take them a while to accept strangers.

With the right training, these dogs make good family pets. Catahoulas need to know that their owners are in charge. Otherwise, they can be destructive or **aggressive** and get into trouble.

These excellent hunters can climb trees!

COAT AND COLOR

The Catahoula leopard dog's coat is short to medium length. It lies flat against the body and does not get **matted** or tangled. This is helpful for a dog that was **bred** to handle rough outdoor conditions.

Some Catahoula leopard dog coats have the distinctive leopard pattern. This beautiful pattern has a base color with spots of at least one other color. Other Catahoulas are solid red, yellow, black, or chocolate. They may also have **brindle** coats.

The Catahoula leopard dog is known for its light blue eyes. But this breed may also have amber, green, or brown eyes. Sometimes, each eye is a different color.

The Catahoula's captivating light blue eyes are also known as glass eyes.

SIZE

Catahoula leopard dogs are medium to medium large. These dogs weigh between 50 and 95 pounds (23 and 43 kg). Males usually stand 22 to 26 inches (56 to 66 cm) tall. Females are about 20 to 24 inches (51 to 61 cm) tall.

This **breed**'s strong build makes it well suited to hunting and herding. The Catahoula leopard dog has a deep, broad chest. Its long, muscular legs are great for running over long distances. Its webbed toes make it a great swimmer. And, they help it work in marshy areas.

The Catahoula leopard dog has a strong, fairly wide **muzzle** with well-developed cheeks. Its eyes are medium sized and its ears are medium length. The

The loyal, hardworking Catahoula leopard dog is the state dog of Louisiana.

ears drop forward and taper to a rounded tip. The tail is thick at the base and also tapers to a tip. The dog carries it upright when alert.

CARE

The Catahoula leopard dog requires a lot of exercise and attention. It needs to go out for a run for at least one hour each day. This active **breed** must have a lot of space to be healthy and happy. It also likes to be around people, not tied up outside all day.

Catahoulas are generally healthy, but they can have serious medical problems. Like many breeds, Catahoulas can suffer from **hip dysplasia** and other joint problems. White dogs or white-faced dogs with glass eyes have a high chance of being **deaf** in one or both ears.

Like all dogs, your Catahoula should see a veterinarian at least once a year. He or she will check your dog's health and provide **vaccines**. The veterinarian will also **spay** or **neuter** your pet. This is important for any dog that is not going to be bred.

Catahoulas are used to working with people. So, these dogs do not like to be alone.

FEEDING

Catahoula leopard dogs need high-quality food to stay active, healthy, and strong. Many owners prefer to feed their dogs dry food. Wet and semimoist foods are also available. A veterinarian or a **breeder** can suggest what and how much food your dog needs.

When first bringing a puppy home, feed it the same food it ate at the breeder's. Change to a new food gradually to avoid causing an upset stomach. A puppy should eat two to three small meals per day. An adult will eat two larger meals every day.

It is important for dogs to have plenty of water. Owners should make sure their Catahoulas always have a bowl of fresh, clean water to drink. These dogs especially need a drink during hot weather or after exercising.

Don't be tempted to feed your dog table scraps. Good-quality commercial food has all the nutrients your dog needs.

THINGS THEY NEED

Catahoula leopard dogs love to be active. So get outside and play with your dog every day! It is important for these dogs to have a large, open area where they can run. A fenced yard or a dog park will help keep them safe outdoors.

Obedience training is important for all dogs. It is especially vital for strong, smart **breeds** like the Catahoula leopard dog. These dogs need to know the rules and learn to obey their owners. Training helps them behave and get along well with people and other dogs.

Catahoulas should have a strong leash and collar. The collar should include license and identification tags. These dogs also need comfortable places to sleep. If your dog sleeps outdoors, it needs a warm doghouse to shelter it from cold and rain. Catahoulas need sturdy food and water bowls, too.

Chew toys will help keep your Catahoula's teeth clean.

PUPPIES

Like all dogs, Catahoula leopard dogs are **pregnant** for about 63 days. Females usually have **litters** of 8 to 12 puppies.

At first, the puppies are completely dependent on their mother. After 10 to 14 days, they can see and hear. Still, they should stay with their mother until they are about eight weeks old. Then, their new owners can take them home.

Owners should **socialize** puppies and give them lots of new experiences. Catahoula leopard dogs especially need to adjust to being around other dogs and people.

A healthy dog can live for 10 to 15 years. So a Catahoula leopard dog will provide years of love and protection for its family.

Is the Catahoula leopard dog the right breed for you?

20

GLOSSARY

aggressive (uh-GREH-sihv) - displaying hostility.

American Kennel Club (AKC) - an organization that studies and promotes interest in purebred dogs.

breed - a group of animals sharing the same ancestors and appearance. A breeder is a person who raises animals. Raising animals is often called breeding them.

brindle - having dark streaks or spots on a gray, tan, or tawny background.

Canidae (KAN-uh-dee) - the scientific Latin name for the dog family. Members of this family are called canids. They include wolves, jackals, foxes, coyotes, and domestic dogs.

deaf - wholly or partly unable to hear.

domesticate - to adapt something to life with humans.

hip dysplasia (HIHP dihs-PLAY-zhuh) - unusual formation of the hip joint.

litter - all of the puppies born at one time to a mother dog.

mat - to form into a tangled mass.

muzzle - an animal's nose and jaws.

neuter (NOO-tuhr) - to remove a male animal's reproductive glands.

pregnant - having one or more babies growing within the body.

socialize - to accustom an animal or a person to spending time with others.

spay - to remove a female animal's reproductive organs.

vaccine (vak-SEEN) - a shot given to prevent illness or disease.

WEB SITES

To learn more about Catahoula leopard dogs, visit ABDO Publishing Company online. Web sites about Catahoula leopard dogs are featured on our Book Links page. These links are routinely monitored and updated to provide the most current information available.

www.abdopublishing.com

23

INDEX